Riding Through the Dark: An Inspirational memoir About Lessons Horses Teach Us About Hope

Finding Mindfulness and Courage, Trust, and Stillness in the Company of Horses

Amber M Wilde

Contents

1. Mounting Up - The Courage to Begin   1
2. Trust and Patience in the Arena   7
3. Falling and Getting Back Up   13
4. The Quiet Bond   19
5. Lessons from the Trail   25
6. When the Barn is Quiet   31
7. The Herd and the Heart   37
8. Riding Through the Dark   43
9. Dismounting with Grace   50

Chapter 1

Mounting Up - The Courage to Begin

Facing the Mounting Block Again

The barn is quiet in the early morning. Sunlight seeps through the gaps in the wooden walls, and the smell of hay and leather fills the space. Somewhere outside, a horse nickers softly.

You stand beside the mounting block, hand resting on the saddle that once felt like home. The reins tremble slightly between your fingers. The memory of falling flashes like a film reel - hooves pounding, a blur of ground and sky, the thud that stole your breath. Your body remembers what your mind would rather forget.

The horse shifts, calm and curious. You feel the tremor in your own hands, a pulse of fear that travels up your arms. Fear, you remind yourself, is not failure. It is a message from the body asking, "Are you safe?" The challenge now is to answer that question with patience rather than panic.

You take a breath. The air smells of earth and cedar shavings. You stroke the horse's neck, feeling warmth under your palm, a heartbeat steady and sure. You are here again. That is the first act of courage.

Understanding Fear and Trauma

Fear after a fall is not weakness. It is biology. Riders who experience trauma often show signs of hyper-arousal - a racing heart, shaking, and heightened alertness - or hypo-arousal, where the body numbs itself, disconnecting from sensation. These reactions are the brain's way of protecting you.

The amygdala, a small almond-shaped structure deep in the brain, acts like an alarm system. It detects threat and floods the body with adrenaline and cortisol, preparing you to fight, flee, or freeze. After an accident, the amygdala can stay on high alert, scanning for danger even in safe environments.

This is why the simplest things can trigger anxiety: the clang of a stirrup, the smell of manure, the sight of the arena where it happened. Each sensory detail reactivates the neural network associated with fear. For some riders, simply tightening the girth or walking past the mounting block is enough to make the body tense. The mind says, "You are fine," but the body whispers, "Not yet."

Recognising these triggers is not a setback. It is information. It tells you where healing must begin.

The Science Behind Fear: What Happens in the Brain

When a fall or frightening event occurs, the amygdala records the emotional intensity of that memory. The hippocampus, another key brain structure, helps place the event in context - when and where it happened. In trauma, the hippocampus can become overwhelmed, meaning the brain stores fragments of sensory memory without proper context. Later, when you see the same arena or smell the same scent, the amygdala reacts as if the fall is happening again.

Understanding this process is liberating. It means your fear is not irrational. It is a physiological echo of survival. The goal of recovery is not to erase the memory but to teach your body that you are safe now.

Rebuilding Confidence: Preparation and Support

Healing begins before you ever put your foot in the stirrup.

Protective preparation: Wearing proper safety gear - a well-fitted helmet, boots with grip, a body protector - signals to your brain that you are ready and safe. Choose a calm environment with a trustworthy horse. Confidence grows in settings that feel predictable and secure.

Supportive coaching: A patient trainer who listens and adjusts goals to your pace is invaluable. Studies show that riders who rebuild confidence successfully do so through small, realistic goals and compassionate guidance rather than pressure.

Gradual re-exposure: Start on the ground. Lunge your horse, watch how they move, walk beside them. When you are ready, mount with a helper nearby. Stay mounted for a few minutes, then dismount before anxiety rises. Incremental exposure teaches the body safety through experience, not words.

Every calm session lays another brick in the bridge back to trust.

Techniques for Managing Fear

Exposure therapy: Controlled exposure helps the brain rewrite the story of fear. Begin with what feels manageable - perhaps standing beside your horse - and progress slowly to mounting, then walking. Each success replaces panic with a new memory of safety.

Cognitive reframing and mindfulness: Horse Journals recommends identifying and challenging catastrophic thoughts. Instead of "I could fall again," replace it with "I am learning to ride with awareness." Pair this reframing with mindfulness techniques. Deep breathing slows the heart rate. A body scan relaxes tense muscles. The more often you pair calmness with the act of riding, the more your brain learns that the saddle is no longer a threat.

Incremental challenges: Stretch your comfort zone gently. Let go of the saddle for a moment, loosen your reins an inch, ride one stride longer than before. Each small act of courage strengthens the neural pathways of confidence. Progress may be slow, but it is steady.

Embracing Vulnerability and Growth

Courage is not the absence of fear. It is the decision to show up despite it.

The first time you mount again, your heart may pound, your breath may quicken, your thoughts may race. That is not failure. That is the body remembering. Courage is what happens when you stay present through that moment.

In the saddle, you learn to accept vulnerability as part of partnership. Horses respond not to perfection but to authenticity. When you steady your breathing, when you choose trust over tension, your horse feels it and mirrors your calm. Together, you relearn balance - both physical and emotional.

Every rider who has fallen carries a private story of recovery. Each return to the mounting block is a quiet act of bravery. It says: I am still here. I am willing to begin again.

Setting the Tone for the Journey

Mounting up after fear is more than a physical act. It is a metaphor for living. To climb back into the saddle is to choose hope over avoidance, presence over paralysis. It is to say, "I will meet my fear with curiosity instead of judgment."

This is where the journey of the book begins. The lessons that follow - on trust, patience, resilience, and connection - are all rooted in this moment of choosing to begin again.

Fear will visit you from time to time, just as it visits every rider, every human. But with support, self-compassion, and a steady hand on the reins, you can move through it. One breath. One step. One ride at a time.

And somewhere between the heartbeat of your horse and your own, you will find the courage that never truly left you.

Chapter 2

Trust and Patience in the Arena

The Unresponsive Horse

He stood in the middle of the arena, head low, eyes distant, a statue carved from chestnut and silence. The more I asked, the less he moved. My heels nudged, my voice called, the reins pressed. Nothing. It was as if every cue dissolved before it reached him.

Frustration rose like heat in my chest. I had learned to make a horse yield through firmness and clarity, yet this one seemed immune. The harder I tried, the more he retreated. His stillness was not defiance; it was resignation. Somewhere along the way, he had learned that human requests came with pressure he could not escape.

That day, I dropped the reins, stepped back, and took a breath. Instead of asking, I waited. The air between us shifted. His ears flicked toward me, his eyes softened. It was the first moment of real connection we had shared. I had stopped trying to control him and started trying to listen.

. . .

The Science of Trust and Emotional Mirroring

Horses are masters of silent communication. As prey animals, their survival depends on reading the smallest shifts in body language, tension, and intent. They sense our internal weather before we speak a word. Horses mirror our emotions through subtle changes in their own posture and expression. A calm human presence invites calmness in the horse. A frustrated rider often finds that frustration reflected right back.

This mirroring is not symbolic. It is physiological. When we enter a horse's space, our nervous systems begin to communicate. Studies cited by Horses and Humans Research Foundation show that horses and humans can synchronise their heart rhythms during quiet interaction. When we slow our breathing and soften our focus, the horse's heart rate often drops too. The electromagnetic field generated by the horse's large heart, which is five times stronger than a human's, can influence our own heart rhythms, reducing anxiety and creating a sense of mutual calm.

Trust is not demanded through dominance but earned through emotional steadiness. The horse reads your truth, not your intention.

Natural Horsemanship: Gentle Pressure and Release

In natural horsemanship, communication is built on clarity and timing. Pressure is used not to punish but to guide, and release is the horse's reward. When a rider applies gentle pressure through reins, seat, or leg and releases it the moment the horse responds, the animal learns that cooperation brings relief. This predictability builds confidence and reduces fear.

The mistake most riders make is holding the pressure too long. Delayed release or excessive insistence confuses the horse, creating anxiety or defensive behaviour. The key is consistency. Every cue must mean the same thing every time. When your communication is fair and reliable, your horse begins to trust that you will not ask for the impossible.

Pressure and release are more than training techniques. They are a conversation about respect. Each cue says, "I see you. I will listen."

Building Emotional Regulation and Self-Worth

Working with horses is as much about managing your own emotions as it is about influencing theirs. Equine-assisted therapy programs described by *Horses and Humans Research Foundation* show that effective handlers cultivate patience, vulnerability, and clear boundaries. Horses thrive under steady energy and become unsettled by emotional volatility. Learning to regulate your breathing, tone, and body language teaches the horse that you are safe to be near.

This emotional steadiness benefits humans as well. According to *Connected Horse*, participants in therapeutic riding programs report improved confidence, self-awareness, and trust. Many describe how horses teach them to let go of perfection and to value progress over control.

Patience in the arena becomes patience in life. When you learn to quiet your own nervous system for the sake of another being, you begin to discover inner strength that force alone could never produce.

Practical Techniques for Trust-Building

Mindful presence: One of the simplest exercises involves standing beside your horse, placing a hand on its chest, and matching your breathing to its rhythm. Research from *Wellpower* and *Horses and Humans* shows that this practice can lower heart rate and cortisol levels in both horse and human. The shared stillness reminds you that trust begins in calm awareness, not action.

Consistent cues: Use your body language deliberately. A soft gaze, steady shoulders, and rhythmic breathing tell your horse that you are clear and confident. Apply light pressure to ask, and release instantly when you feel the smallest try. Horses learn through relief, not repetition.

Observation and reflection: Keep sessions short and finish on a positive note. Notice how the horse's ears, eyes, and posture change with your energy. Journal after each ride. Ask yourself: When did my horse relax? When did tension rise? What does that reveal about my own emotions?

Each interaction becomes a mirror. Each reflection is an opportunity to grow.

Balancing Control and Connection

True partnership is found in the balance between guidance and freedom. When we stop striving to dominate and start seeking to understand, a horse begins to offer more than compliance; it offers willingness. Control without connection creates resistance. Connection without structure creates chaos. Trust lives in the middle, where leadership is grounded in empathy and consistency.

This lesson extends far beyond the arena. In relationships, parenting, or leadership, we face the same choice: demand obedience or invite cooperation. Horses remind us that influence built on respect endures far longer than power enforced through fear.

When we slow down, breathe, and allow space for response, we discover that communication is not about command but about listening deeply enough to be heard.

Trust as a Shared Journey

Trust cannot be rushed. It unfolds through repetition, patience, and honesty. Every feed bucket carried, every grooming session, every quiet moment of waiting by the gate teaches the horse that you are safe. Over time, the small gestures accumulate into something profound - a bond grounded in reliability and care.

To trust a horse is to trust yourself. It is to believe that gentleness is strength and that patience is power. The same courage that brought you back to the saddle will guide you in building this connection.

In the stillness of the arena, two heartbeats find the same rhythm. The horse breathes out, and you breathe with it. The distance between fear and peace becomes no more than the space of a single breath shared between species who, in their own ways, are both learning to trust again.

Chapter 3

Falling and Getting Back Up

The Fall

It happened in a heartbeat. One moment, the rhythm of hooves carried me forward in perfect balance. The next, the world tilted. The ground rose fast and unforgiving. I remember the sound first—the sharp slap of dust against my helmet, the startled snort of the horse, the ringing silence that followed.

For a moment I just lay there, breath caught between disbelief and pain. The sun glared through the dust, turning the arena into a golden haze. My body trembled, but my mind felt distant, as if watching someone else fall. That single instant, so small and yet so immense, became the doorway to every lesson that would follow.

Every rider has a fall that humbles them. Sometimes it happens in the saddle. Sometimes it happens in life. Either way, the ground always feels the same: hard, real, and honest.

· · ·

Shock and Silence

After a fall, the body speaks before the mind can understand. Hands shake. The heart races. Or sometimes everything goes still, as if the air itself has frozen. Fear and trauma often manifest in two distinct ways: hyper-arousal, where the body floods with adrenaline, or hypo-arousal, where it numbs to survive.

I felt both. My heart galloped while my limbs refused to move. My breath came in short bursts that barely reached my lungs. I stared at the dirt beside me and thought, absurdly, of how it smelled like clay and sweat and endings.

These reactions are not weakness. They are the body's ancient wisdom at work, the same instinct that tells a prey animal when to run or freeze. Trauma is simply the nervous system doing its best to keep us safe.

"I felt the ground go still beneath me," I later wrote in my journal, "but my heart ran on like a startled horse."

The Brain's Memory of Fear

The mind has its own way of holding onto the fall. The amygdala, a small part of the brain that manages fear, works like a fire alarm. Once it has been triggered, it stays alert, waiting for any sign of smoke. *Brave Minds Psychological Services* describes this process as hyper-focus on safety after trauma. The brain becomes a watchtower, scanning for anything that looks or feels like danger.

I often thought my mind was like a galloping horse, full of energy but without a rider. A gust of wind or the creak of leather could set my pulse racing. Even when logic told me I was fine, my body said otherwise.

Remembering a fall can reignite the same fear that caused it. This is not a flaw; it is a protective reflex. Your body remembers because it loves you. It wants to keep you alive. The task is to teach it that the danger has passed.

Recognising Triggers and Patterns

Sometimes, it was the smell of liniment that brought my heart to my throat. Other times, the way sunlight slanted across a certain corner of the arena. Sensory triggers - sights, sounds, and smells - can awaken dormant fear circuits.

Once, weeks after my fall, I froze while simply tightening a girth. I had not expected it, which made it worse. My fingers trembled, and shame followed close behind. But awareness became my lifeline. I began to see these moments not as proof of failure but as signals pointing toward where healing was needed.

Awareness is the gentlest of reins. It does not pull or force. It simply guides you to see where your heart is still holding its breath.

Reframing the Fall

In the horse world, falling is inevitable. How we frame it determines what it means. According to equestrian psychologists cited in *The Horse,* riders who reframe falls as lessons recover confidence more quickly than those who see them as failures.

At first, I carried my fall like a secret wound. Then one afternoon, my coach told me to laugh at it. "If you ride long enough," she said, "the ground will know your name. It's not the fall that matters, it's how you rise."

The words stayed with me. Over time, I began to see the fall not as the end of courage but as its beginning. *Brené Brown* reminds us that shame thrives in silence. *Temple Grandin* teaches that fear dissolves through understanding. Falling reveals where trust needs tending - both in the horse and in ourselves.

Healing Through Connection

After every fall, there is a moment when someone reaches for your hand. Maybe it is a trainer, maybe a friend, maybe your horse lowering his head to breathe near your shoulder. That touch carries more power than any spoken reassurance.

Supportive coaching and realistic goals help riders rebuild confidence. A calm voice at the mounting block, a steadying presence at your side, can quiet the alarm bells inside your chest. I remember one friend who said, "You don't have to ride today. Just sit here with him." That small kindness became the first step back.

It is easier to stand when someone steadies the stirrup.

Techniques for Getting Back Up

Breathing and mindfulness: Deep belly breathing tells the nervous system that it is safe to relax. Slow, rhythmic breaths lower heart rate and reduce the body's stress response. I learned to place one hand on my chest and one on my horse's shoulder, matching my inhale to his exhale until both rhythms aligned.

Exposure therapy: According to *Dr. Bridget Walker*, gradual exposure to feared situations helps the brain rewrite its fear memory. The first time, I only sat in the saddle for a minute. The next time, we walked a few steps. By the third session, I could trot without holding my breath. Small steps retrain the brain far better than forcing a leap.

Cognitive reframing: Rewriting our inner script changes everything. "I failed" becomes "I learned." "I'm afraid" becomes "I am aware." Words shape thought, and thought shapes confidence.

Falling taught me that progress is rarely dramatic. It is often a quiet accumulation of small victories.

Riding Through Setbacks

Fear does not disappear; it transforms. Courage is the act of meeting it again and again until it becomes familiar - the ability to stay present and act even when the body still trembles.

I once watched another rider, a young girl who had taken a hard fall, whisper to her horse before mounting again. "We can do this," she told him softly, her hands shaking as she gathered the reins. The gelding flicked an ear, then stepped forward as if he understood. Her bravery that day was not loud, but it was real.

Getting back on the horse mirrors getting back up in life. Both require faith that the fall does not define you. Balance is not the absence of motion; it is the dance between letting go and holding on.

The Wisdom of Falling

Every fall teaches what staying upright cannot. It strips away the illusion of control and replaces it with humility and awareness. The scars, visible or hidden, are not proof of failure but of survival.

In time, the memory of the fall becomes softer. You begin to see it not as the end of something, but as a teacher disguised as gravity.

In falling, we meet the ground. In rising, we meet ourselves anew. And when we climb back into the saddle, we carry not just courage but compassion—for the horse, for the fear, and for the tender parts of ourselves that are still learning to stand.

Chapter 4
The Quiet Bond

Silence Shared

The morning light is soft and pale, filtered through the slats of the barn. Frost still clings to the windows, and the breath of each horse rises like a small cloud in the chill air. The rhythmic sound of hay being chewed fills the space, steady and grounding. I stand beside my horse, one hand resting on his neck, feeling the slow warmth of life beneath my palm.

For a long while, neither of us moves. The silence is full, not empty. His breathing deepens, and mine follows. The steady rise and fall of his ribs becomes a metronome that quiets my racing thoughts.

In that stillness, no words are needed. The connection feels older than language, as if our hearts are having a conversation that our minds are too loud to hear. Some bonds are built not through instruction or effort, but through shared quiet—an understanding that exists simply because both beings are willing to be still together.

. . .

Mindful Presence and Co-Regulation

Horses live entirely in the present. Their awareness is unfiltered and complete. Their survival as prey animals has made them masters at reading energy and body language. They sense our emotional states before we speak. The slightest tension in a shoulder or change in breath tells them everything they need to know.

When we are anxious, they move away. When we soften, they exhale. In their presence, our hidden emotions become visible. They show us what we are feeling before we admit it to ourselves.

During calm, connected interaction, the heart rhythms of humans and horses can become aligned. This heart-rate coherence happens most strongly when people express positive feelings or simply sit quietly beside the horse. Scientists believe the horse's large electromagnetic field can influence human physiology, lowering stress and promoting calm.

In simple terms, it is as if the horse lends us its rhythm. The frantic human heartbeat slows to match the steady pulse of an animal that lives entirely in the moment.

Communicating Without Words

Horses speak volumes without ever making a sound. Their language is written in the flick of an ear, the shift of weight, the blink of an eye. To communicate well with them, we must learn to observe with patience.

There was a day when my horse turned his head slightly toward me, one ear forward, one back. I realised he was reflecting my own hesitation. My shoulders had tensed without me noticing, and he had mirrored that uncertainty. When I exhaled and let my body soften, he sighed too, the tension dissolving in both of us.

This silent feedback loop is what makes equine work so transformative. *Tufts University's Cummings School of Veterinary Medicine* has studied equine-assisted learning programs and found that participants develop greater confidence, communication, and coping skills. These lessons arise not from words but from awareness-recognising how our energy influences another being and adjusting with compassion.

The Science of Quiet - Heartbeats in Harmony

Dr. Ann Baldwin and other researchers have explored the phenomenon of physiological synchrony between humans and horses. Heart-rate frequencies often match during interaction, with the human heart following the lead of the horse's rhythm. The result is a shared calm, a state where both species seem to rest in mutual trust.

This alignment is more than a poetic idea; it has measurable effects. When coherence occurs, both horse and human experience reduced stress levels. The bond becomes a biological conversation, one heartbeat echoing another until both settle into stillness.

Your heart, once racing with anxiety, begins to slow. You feel the tension release from your shoulders. The horse beside you lowers his head, eyelids soft, and together you find peace in a rhythm older than thought.

From Silence to Insight - Emotional Awareness

Mindful grooming became my first meditation. With each slow brushstroke, I noticed the shine of the coat, the warmth beneath the hair, the way the brush hummed softly across muscle. The act of grooming became a dialogue of trust: each movement a question, each response a quiet yes.

Mindful interaction as a path to empathy and gratitude. When you slow down enough to notice the texture of a mane or the rhythm of breath, you begin to sense your own inner stillness returning.

In those moments, the horse is both teacher and mirror. He reflects how present you are. If your thoughts drift, his ears flick. If your breathing quickens, his muscles tighten. But when you focus on the now—when you let gratitude replace distraction—he relaxes, and so do you.

Temple Grandin reminds us that to truly understand animals, we must step into their sensory world. To see through their eyes is to learn empathy in its purest form. And as *Brené Brown* might say, vulnerability in this context is not weakness but openness - the willingness to feel and to connect without walls.

Practical Guidance – Nurturing the Quiet Bond

Silent companionship: Spend time with your horse without an agenda. Leave the halter off if it is safe. Simply stand nearby, breathe, and observe. Place a hand on the horse's chest and match your breathing to his. The body will naturally attune, and calm will follow.

Mindful grooming: Use grooming as a meditative practice. Notice each stroke, the texture of the brush, the warmth of the horse's skin. Stay aware of your breath and posture.

Listening with the body: Learn to read the subtleties—ears moving toward or away, eyes soft or hard, muscles rippling beneath the surface. Respond with patience and curiosity rather than command.

Keep a journal of these moments. Record what changes inside you when you allow silence to lead. Over time, you may find that the lessons learned in the barn spill quietly into the rest of your life.

Connection Beyond the Barn

The quiet bond does not end when you leave the stable. Its wisdom carries into every conversation and relationship. When we learn to listen with our whole selves - to offer presence rather than advice - we create safety for others to do the same.

The art of listening without interruption, of letting silence speak before we do, is as healing among people as it is with horses. In both worlds, connection thrives when we stop trying to fill the air and instead learn to inhabit it together.

Trust and patience are not skills confined to reins and hooves. They are the foundation of every meaningful relationship.

The Echo of Heartbeats

There are moments in the barn when everything feels suspended: no words, no tasks, only breath and heartbeat and the sound of hay being chewed in rhythm with the earth itself. In those moments, you realise that the horse has been teaching you all along—to be still, to listen, to return to your own centre.

Perhaps the greatest gift horses give us is not their power or their speed, but their willingness to stand beside us quietly. In their company, we remember that peace is not something we must chase. It is something we find when we finally stop moving long enough to feel it.

In the quiet between heartbeats, we come home - to the horse, to the present, to ourselves.

Chapter 5

Lessons from the Trail

Setting Out on the Path

Morning mist drifts low across the meadow, clinging to the dew-laden grass. The air is crisp and filled with the scent of earth and pine. I adjust the reins and feel the warmth of my horse beneath me, muscles shifting in quiet readiness. His ears flick forward, listening to the rustle of leaves and the faint hum of waking birds.

The first step onto the trail always feels like a threshold. Hooves press softly into the soil, a rhythm steady and sure. The forest opens ahead, a green corridor filled with the unknown. The path winds into places I cannot yet see, asking me to trust both my horse and myself.

Each ride begins as an outward journey, but quickly becomes something inward. The trail stretches ahead like a mirror for the mind, reflecting courage, patience, and the willingness to be present. Every hoofbeat is both movement and meditation, carrying me deeper into a landscape that asks only this: to breathe, to listen, and to let go.

The Physiology of Calm - How Horses and Trails Heal

Science affirms what riders have long felt. Simply being near a horse slows the breath and steadies the heart. It is well known that interaction with horses can lower cortisol, the body's primary stress hormone, and promote relaxation. The natural rhythm of the horse's movement mirrors our own physiology, inviting balance where tension once lived.

When humans and horses spend quiet time together, their heart rhythms can synchronise. The horse's large electromagnetic field, stronger than a human's, can influence and steady our heartbeat, easing anxiety and promoting calm.

On the trail, this connection feels tangible. With every step, my body finds its rhythm in his. The sway of the saddle, the sound of breathing, the pulse beneath my legs-each element becomes part of a shared tempo. In that synchrony, thought softens and the chatter of the mind fades. There is no need to hurry. The trail itself becomes a kind of therapy.

Mindfulness on the Trail - Present Moment Awareness

As we move deeper into the forest, I begin to notice everything. The sound of hooves muffled by pine needles. The scent of sun-warmed resin. The faint clicking of grasshoppers. The leather of the reins feels smooth beneath my fingers, and the rhythm of my breathing matches the rise and fall of his shoulders.

Horses mirror human emotions. When I am distracted, my horse slows, uncertain. When I centre myself and focus on the present, his stride lengthens and steadies. Riding becomes an act of mindfulness. It asks me to pay attention—not only to the trail but to the energy I bring into the moment.

Mindfulness is not about emptying the mind; it is about filling it with awareness. On the trail, there is no room for the past or future. There is only the scent of pine, the hum of insects, the heartbeat beneath you. In this simplicity, peace quietly returns.

Nature as Co-Therapist

Even twenty minutes spent in nature can reduce stress hormones. When you combine that with time spent with a horse, the effects multiply. The natural world grounds you, while the horse provides companionship without judgment.

Trail riding is a unique form of therapy because it allows movement through both space and emotion. The forest becomes a sanctuary, the horse a guide. Studies from *Utah State University Extension* highlight that equine programs conducted outdoors can enhance mental health, especially for those unable to access traditional nature-based therapies like hiking. The horse becomes your bridge to the earth.

As we climb a hill, I feel the muscles beneath me working in harmony with mine. The wind brushes my face, and the landscape stretches wide and forgiving. Nature, it seems, has always known how to heal us. Horses simply remind us to slow down enough to notice.

· · ·

Balancing on Uneven Ground – Physical and Emotional Benefits

The trail twists and turns, sometimes smooth, sometimes rocky. Each step demands subtle adjustments - a shift of weight here, a softening of hands there. Navigating varied terrain engages the rider's core and improves posture, while also developing the horse's balance and fitness.

But beyond the physical, there is a deeper lesson. The uneven ground mirrors life's unpredictability. One moment the footing is solid, the next it gives way to sand or stone. In those moments, trust becomes more important than control. The horse feels your hesitation instantly. If you tense, he hesitates too. If you breathe and stay centred, he steps forward with confidence.

Every small recovery on the trail teaches resilience. The art of riding through rough patches - staying relaxed yet responsive - translates directly to how we navigate uncertainty in life.

The Horse as Guide - Trust and Connection

Midway through the ride, we reach a narrow stream. The water glimmers with sunlight, rippling over stones. My horse pauses, lowering his head to inspect it. For a moment, he snorts softly, unsure. I could push him forward, but instead I wait. I let him think.

He takes a breath, then steps through. His trust in me has been earned, not demanded. Horses teach that leadership is not about force; it is about patience and mutual confidence.

When I keep my emotions steady, he mirrors that calm. When I rush or tighten, he senses the discord immediately.

Hoses are emotional barometers. They feel what we feel. Learning to regulate our own state in the saddle - staying grounded even when the path is unpredictable - builds not only better horsemanship but greater emotional intelligence.

Trails and Life's Darker Paths - Metaphorical Insights

Sometimes the trail narrows and disappears into shadow. The air cools, the light dims, and the path ahead is uncertain. These stretches remind me of life's darker passages - the moments when we cannot see the way forward but must keep moving anyway.

Riding through such spaces requires faith: in your horse, in your instincts, in the quiet rhythm that continues even when vision fails. The discipline of keeping your seat on uneven ground mirrors the discipline of staying steady through grief, anxiety, or doubt.

The lessons of the trail echo far beyond the ride itself. Every rock and root becomes a metaphor. Balance. Patience. Presence. The same qualities that keep you upright in the saddle will also carry you through the shifting terrain of life.

Staying balanced with a horse is a practice in hope. It is a reminder that calm can coexist with uncertainty, and that courage often looks like simply continuing on.

The Journey Continues

The trail opens into a clearing. Sunlight filters through the trees, and the sound of birds returns. My horse flicks an ear back toward me, waiting for direction. We pause together, breathing in the quiet satisfaction of miles well traveled.

The lessons linger long after the ride ends. The scent of the forest, the steady rhythm of hoofbeats, and the shared calm between rider and horse become part of you. They remind you that balance is not about perfection - it is about presence.

Every path we take, whether on horseback or in life, asks the same question: Can you stay open? Can you trust the journey even when you do not know where it leads?

Perhaps that is the greatest lesson the trail offers. Within each ride lies a gentle wisdom, waiting for those willing to listen. The journey continues, both outward and inward, one quiet step at a time.

Chapter 6
When the Barn is Quiet

Dawn Light and Soft Whinnies

The world feels suspended just before sunrise, the chill in the air carrying the promise of morning. My boots crunch softly on the frost as I walk toward the barn. The wooden doors creak open and, inside, the horses stir. One shifts his weight; another nickers in greeting.

Dust motes drift lazily through the light filtering down from the rafters, and the smell of hay fills the air - warm, sweet, grounding. There is something holy about these moments. The barn holds a kind of quiet that is not empty but full: full of breath, of warmth, of presence. Inside there is only rhythm and rest - the soft munch of hay - while the outside world feels far away.

Time slows here. The rush of thought dissolves, leaving space for stillness. In its quiet way, the barn teaches us how to breathe again.

· · ·

The Power of Stillness - A Research-Backed Sanctuary

When I read studies on cortisol and heart rate, I realised that science was only confirming what every horse person already knows in their bones: being with horses heals.

Equine-assisted activities have been shown to lower cortisol, the body's primary stress hormone, while improving mood and overall well-being. Simply standing near a calm horse can slow the pulse and quiet the mind.

Feeding, grooming, or even leaning on a stall door invites complete presence, turning the barn into a sanctuary. Every movement - a hand brushing a coat, a halter clipped softly into place - requires mindfulness. This quiet attentiveness fosters emotional regulation and offers a mental reset for anyone navigating stress or grief.

Within these walls, there is no demand to explain or perform. Horses do not ask for words; they respond to energy, truth, and tone. Their steadiness offers safety, and their acceptance creates room for release. The barn becomes both mirror and refuge - a place where emotion can surface and soften without judgment.

Horses as Mirrors and Healers

Horses live completely in the present moment. They do not dwell on what has passed or worry about what might come. Their calm presence invites us to slow down and match their rhythm. When we approach them with tension, they step away; when we breathe deeply and settle, they return.

This mirroring is not only emotional - it's physiological. Research shared by *Wellpower* describes how a horse's large electromagnetic field can influence human heart rate, promoting relaxation and reducing stress. Placing a hand on a horse's chest and breathing in rhythm can bring both human and horse into shared calm.

I have stood this way many mornings - hand resting on the warm rise of a palomino's shoulder, my breath syncing with hers. The quiet exchange feels like a conversation beyond words. In that silent communion, healing begins.

Embracing the Five Senses - A Mindfulness Practice

In the barn, every sense is invited to participate. You can hear the crunch of hay, the soft snort of contentment, the gentle creak of wooden beams. You can smell the earthy sweetness of straw and leather. You can feel the velvet of a muzzle brushing your palm, the warmth of a flank against your shoulder.

When you slow down enough to notice, gratitude blooms. Simply pausing to listen to horses chew hay can reshape emotion and open the heart to thankfulness.

I remember one winter morning when the world outside was frozen and still. Inside, the barn glowed golden with lamplight. The sound of chewing, the quiet rustle of shavings, the rhythm of breath—all of it seemed to dissolve my worries. For a moment, time itself exhaled.

Mindfulness and Flow - Why Barn Time Matters

Riding instructors often say that a good ride begins long before you mount the horse. The quiet work in the barn - the brushing, the breathing, the listening - sets the tone. Connecting with a horse through these small rituals resets the mind, easing stress and bringing focus back into the body.

Each brushstroke, each adjusted buckle, becomes its own meditation. The rhythmic motions of grooming and saddling tell the nervous system that it is safe. In these moments, thought slows and presence takes over.

The barn is a perfect place to practice mindfulness in motion. These simple, deliberate actions build empathy and strengthen the unspoken language between horse and human. When we are fully present, horses sense it - and reward it - with trust.

Patience grows naturally here. So does compassion. Connection cannot be rushed; it unfolds quietly, like dawn light spreading over a sleeping field.

Gratitude and Reflection - Journaling in the Barn

When the chores are done, I like to sit on a hay bale with a small notebook in hand. The horses move softly in their stalls, and I write about what I notice - the smell of the barn, the steady rhythm of chewing, the way peace feels in my body.

Writing here turns observation into gratitude. Describing the sensations and emotions of barn life deepens awareness, helping carry the lesson of stillness beyond these walls.

Reflection transforms release into growth, creating balance between mind and heart.

In the barn's quiet, honesty comes easier—with myself, with the page, with the past. Vulnerability feels less like a risk and more like a return. The horses do not mind if you cry or sit in silence. They only ask that you stay present.

Extending Quiet Lessons Beyond the Barn

What we learn in the stillness of the barn applies everywhere. The pause before a ride becomes the pause before a difficult conversation. The patience we practice with a nervous horse softens our tone with those we love.

The mindfulness of the barn follows us into daily life - a reminder to breathe before reacting, to listen before speaking, to notice beauty even in small, ordinary things.

The promise of this book lives here: in learning to listen, to stay balanced, and to find strength through presence. The lessons the horse teaches in stillness are the same lessons life asks of us when chaos returns—to stay steady, to breathe, to trust the rhythm.

The Barn as a Sanctuary

As the sun climbs higher, golden light spills through the open door. Horses begin to shift toward the pasture, hooves echoing softly against the floor. I linger a moment longer, reluctant to leave.

My heartbeat slows. My thoughts soften. I walk out carrying more than hay on my clothes - I carry the stillness itself.

Perhaps this is what the horses have been teaching all along: that peace is not found in doing, but in being. The barn reminds us that within every pause lies an invitation to return to ourselves.

In the gentle quiet of morning, among the soft whinnies and drifting dust, we remember that silence is not empty. It is full - of life, of grace, of beginnings.

Chapter 7
The Herd and the Heart

Watching the Herd at Dusk

Evening settles gently over the pasture. The air is golden and still, filled with the low hum of insects and the soft swish of tails brushing away flies. A few horses stand side by side, their heads lowered, grazing in quiet harmony. One flicks an ear; another answers with a shift of weight. Their language is silent but complete.

The herd moves as if choreographed, though no one seems to be giving orders. Each horse knows its place, not from fear but from familiarity. The rhythm of their companionship is steady and soothing, like waves against a shore. Standing at the fence, I feel like an invited guest at a secret gathering. The calm that settles over them begins to settle over me too.

Here, belonging has no words. It is written in gestures, in presence, in the simple act of standing together as the sun slips behind the trees.

· · ·

The Web of Social Bonds - Stress Relief and Security

Horses are deeply social creatures. Their lives depend on connection. In the wild and in domestic herds, relationships form the fabric of safety and peace. Research shows that stable herd bonds can last for years, reducing stress and fostering security. When relationships are balanced, the entire group remains calm and cohesive.

When a herd member is removed, the disruption is profound. Studies have documented how mares vocalise, pace, and show elevated heart rates when separated from companions. Their vigilance increases, revealing how essential social ties are to emotional stability.

Isolation, by contrast, is harmful. Solitary horses experience increased cortisol levels, compromised immunity, and even depression-like symptoms. They may develop repetitive behaviours such as weaving or stall walking—signs of emotional distress.

Connection is not optional for horses; it is survival. And in that truth lies a lesson for us.

The Language of Horses - Subtle Cues and Mutual Grooming

Horses communicate constantly, though rarely with sound. a Flick of an ear, a swish of a tail, or a small shift in stance can send messages to the entire herd. Their communication is so refined that it often passes unnoticed by human eyes.

Among the most intimate gestures is mutual grooming. Two horses stand close, necks curved toward each other, gently nibbling along withers and shoulders. It looks simple, but it is profound. During grooming, heart rates drop and endorphins are released, creating feelings of relaxation and trust. Horses do not groom just anyone; they choose their closest companions for this ritual.

Even the occasional squeal or pinned ear has purpose. These small confrontations maintain order and respect. Such moments are rarely aggressive - they are corrections, not cruelty. The herd keeps peace through communication, not control.

Dominance, Leadership and Non-Linear Hierarchies

Human culture often misunderstands the word "dominance." In a horse herd, it is not about bullying or aggression. Dominance simply determines access to resources and maintains stability. Age, experience, and confidence often matter more than size or strength.

Researchers have observed that herd hierarchies are not strictly linear. There is usually a top dominant horse, but leadership shifts depending on the situation. A confident mare might lead the herd to water, while another decides when to move to shelter. Leadership, in this sense, is fluid and earned through trust.

Natural leadership is cooperative. No single horse is always in charge. Authority emerges through consistency and calm decision-making, not force. Horses follow those who make them feel safe.

It is a model of leadership that many human groups could learn from: gentle authority grounded in empathy and reliability.

Subgroups and Friendships - The Importance of Choice

Within every herd are smaller bands - pairs or trios bound by friendship. Horses choose companions based on temperament, age, and shared experience. These friendships are easy to spot: the horses graze side by side, move together, and often rest with their bodies touching.

These chosen relationships are vital to a horse's emotional health. Friends groom each other, stand watch, and sometimes even protect one another during conflicts. Group stability and adequate space strengthen these bonds. Conversely, frequent regrouping, competition for food, or overcrowding can fracture them.

Watching a herd, you begin to recognize the quiet constancy of friendship. It is not loud or dramatic; it is a gentle promise to stand near, to listen, to trust.

Lessons in Belonging - What Humans Can Learn

The herd's harmony offers a blueprint for human belonging. Within the group, individuality is respected, yet each member is part of something greater. Horses remind us that true belonging does not require uniformity - it asks for acceptance and balance.

Mutual grooming in horses mirrors our own acts of care: a reassuring word, a shared laugh, a hand offered without expectation. Small gestures build trust and lower stress, whether among horses or humans.

Leadership in the herd is cooperative, not controlling. Force fractures trust. The same is true for us. The best leaders, human or horse, are those who listen deeply, communicate clearly, and make decisions for the good of the group.

If we study the herd, we begin to see our own reflection. Community thrives on respect, patience, and presence - the same ingredients that keep horses calm and connected.

Practical Reflections - Applying Herd Wisdom

Spend time watching horses interact. Notice who initiates grooming, who stands closest to whom, and how disagreements resolve. You will see a living lesson in emotional intelligence. Conflicts rarely last long; boundaries are established and then forgotten.

Reflect on your own "herd"—your family, your team, your circle of friends. Ask yourself: Do I listen more than I assert? Do I give space for others to find their balance? Do I contribute to calm or to tension?

From a practical standpoint, the same principles that keep a herd healthy can strengthen human groups. Respect established relationships, provide enough space for individuality, and minimize unnecessary disruptions. A peaceful herd—equine or human—thrives on consistency, kindness, and trust.

. . .

The Heart of the Herd

Dusk deepens, and the pasture glows with the last light of day. The horses begin to drift closer together, their bodies forming a loose circle. Some stand head to tail, whisking away flies in quiet cooperation. Others simply rest, one hind leg cocked, eyes half closed.

The scene is ordinary, yet it feels sacred. Here, connection is not forced. It simply exists. Each horse knows it belongs. Each breath, each flick of a tail, contributes to the rhythm of peace.

As I lean against the fence, I feel my own heartbeat slow to match the herd's gentle tempo. The lesson is clear. We are not meant to journey alone. The strength we seek often lives in the spaces between us—in the quiet reassurance of shared presence.

The herd reminds us that hope grows in community, that trust is built through constancy, and that balance is found not in isolation but in belonging. In their calm companionship, we see the reflection of what it means to be human: to listen, to lead with empathy, and to stand together through life's uneven ground.

Chapter 8
Riding Through the Dark

In the Shadow of Loss

The night was cold enough to sting. Frost rimed the fence rails, and a thin mist hung above the pasture. I walked to the barn with my hands shoved into my coat pockets, my breath rising in small clouds. My chest felt hollow, my thoughts heavy. Grief has a way of distorting time. Every step felt slow, stretched thin by memories that refused to quiet down.

Inside, the barn lights were dim. My horse lifted his head at the sound of the door and exhaled softly, his breath white against the chill. For a moment, I just stood there, not ready to move closer. Then, without judgment or hesitation, he took a step toward me. His eyes were soft and steady, holding a kind of knowing that words could not reach.

I pressed my forehead against his neck. His warmth seeped into me, and my breathing began to match his. In that shared silence, something fragile shifted. The weight of sadness did not disappear, but a thread of calm wove through it. The dark remained, yet it no longer felt endless. The quiet presence of a horse had opened a door back toward hope.

A Path through PTSD and Depression - Evidence of Healing

For many, the bond I felt that night is more than emotional - it is therapeutic. Equine-assisted therapy is now a recognised intervention for trauma, grief, and depression. At *Columbia University*, a study involving sixty-three veterans with post-traumatic stress disorder found that weekly sessions co-led by therapists and equine specialists significantly reduced both PTSD symptoms and depression at the end of treatment and again three months later.

Dr. Yuval Neria, one of the study's directors, explains that both veterans and horses share deep concerns about trust and safety. Horses are prey animals, alert to danger and constantly reading their environment. Trauma survivors, too, often live in heightened vigilance. Working with horses allows participants to rebuild trust - first with the animal, then within themselves. They learn to identify emotions, regulate responses, and reestablish confidence in their own intuition.

For many participants, traditional therapy had reached a limit. Sitting in a chair and talking about pain could only go so far. But the experience of standing beside a thousand-pound creature, watching it respond honestly to your presence, sparks transformation. The horse becomes both mirror and mentor, guiding people toward healing that begins in the body and ripples through the heart.

. . .

Beyond the Battlefield - Broad Benefits for Mental Health

The healing power of horses extends beyond trauma recovery. According to *PTSD UK*, equine-assisted therapy fosters patience, empathy, safety, and respect. These qualities grow naturally in the company of horses, whose non-judgmental presence offers refuge from self-criticism and fear.

Studies reveal that equine therapy reduces anxiety, stabilises mood, and cultivates feelings of peace and contentment. A 2016 Norwegian study of participants recovering from substance-use disorders found that time spent with horses provided a renewed sense of identity, purpose, and motivation *(cumberlandheights.org)*. Being outdoors, connected to both horse and nature, anchored participants in the present moment—the only place where true healing occurs.

Horses do not demand explanations. They do not analyse or advise. Instead, they respond to authenticity. Their stillness invites honesty, their sensitivity encourages awareness, and their patience teaches self-control. Interacting with horses helps individuals regulate emotions, develop confidence, and rebuild their ability to connect with others. In the barn, vulnerability becomes strength.

Horses as Mirrors and Teachers

A horse's sensitivity to emotion makes it a living reflection of our internal world. One participant in a *PTSD UK* program described it perfectly: "The horse read everything I was feeling. I realised I had to calm myself before I could ask him to trust me."

When anger, fear, or sadness arise, the horse mirrors those emotions immediately. It may step away, lower its head, or refuse to move forward. These reactions are not rejection; they are reminders. To connect, we must first become congruent—what we feel must align with what we project.

In this way, equine therapy gently dismantles pretence. You cannot hide behind a smile or a story. The horse responds only to truth. Working with them becomes a practice of authenticity, compassion, and self-regulation. They teach us to listen to our bodies, to notice our breath, and to replace control with presence.

Heart Resonance - The Science of Calm

Beyond emotion, there is a measurable physiological connection between humans and horses. Horses emit a powerful electromagnetic field from their heart, many times larger than a human's. When people stand near horses, this field can influence heart rate and rhythm, lowering blood pressure and cortisol levels.

The simple act of placing a hand on a horse's chest and breathing in sync can create measurable coherence between human and equine heartbeats. The rhythm slows, the nervous system calms, and both beings enter a state of quiet harmony.

Many participants in equine therapy report that these moments of connection—standing in silence, hand against a warm chest, feeling the shared pulse—bring peace unlike any other form of meditation. The horse becomes a bridge between the physical and the emotional, the seen and the unseen.

Lessons in Trust, Vulnerability and Hope

To work with a horse is to practice trust every time you step into the arena. Horses respond to clarity and consistency. If you approach them with tension, they retreat; if you move with calm intent, they follow. This dynamic mirrors human relationships in their truest form: genuine, responsive, and rooted in respect.

Equine therapy does not replace traditional counselling. Rather, it complements it by providing a physical, experiential dimension to healing. Trained therapists help translate each interaction into insight—how a moment of fear relates to a deeper wound, or how a breakthrough in communication can extend to family or work.

Healing, like horsemanship, is not a straight line. It unfolds in small, imperfect steps. Some days you ride forward; other days you simply stand beside the horse, breathing through the ache. Both are progress. Both are courage.

Practical Steps - Finding Light in Dark Moments

For readers walking through their own darkness, the lessons of equine connection can become personal rituals of resilience.

Breathing with a Horse: When sorrow feels unbearable, stand quietly beside a horse. Place your hand on its chest and breathe slowly until your heartbeat begins to steady.

Mindful Grooming: Brush your horse with attention and care. Feel the warmth of its coat, the texture of the hair, the rhythm of each stroke. This simple act grounds you in the present.

Guided Sessions: If deeper healing is needed, seek a therapist trained in equine-assisted therapy. Professional guidance ensures safety and helps integrate the lessons into daily life.

Journaling After Barn Time: Write about what you noticed—the horse's eyes, your breathing, the emotions that rose and fell. Reflection transforms experience into understanding.

Each of these practices honours one truth: healing does not rush. It moves like the slow rhythm of hoofbeats in the dark, steady and sure.

Hope as a Practice

Later that same night, I step outside the barn. The moon is higher now, and the air has warmed slightly. My horse stands by the fence, his silhouette silver against the field. I reach out and touch his shoulder one last time before leaving.

The darkness is still there, but it no longer feels empty. His steady breath reminds me that life continues, one heartbeat at a time. The journey through grief is not about erasing pain; it is about learning to move with it, to carry it with gentleness rather than resistance.

This is the promise at the heart of our partnership with horses: by learning to listen, to trust, and to stay balanced beside them, we find our way back to hope. Even in the darkest rides, there is light—quiet, persistent, waiting to be seen.

In the company of a horse, we remember that we are never truly alone.

Chapter 9
Dismounting with Grace

The Last Ride

The sun was low, a pale gold ribbon stretching across the pasture. My horse walked slowly, each step deliberate, his ears flicking back toward me as if to ask if I was still there. His coat caught the light like burnished copper, and the familiar rhythm of his stride carried both comfort and ache.

We moved together in silence. The fields that once felt endless now seemed smaller, framed by memory and time. I could feel his breath beneath my knees, the rise and fall of an old friend whose body had grown tired. I knew, though I did not want to, that this would be our last ride.

When I dismounted, my legs trembled - not from fear, but from the weight of letting go. I pressed my face into his mane, inhaling the scent of hay and dust and years of shared trust. Gratitude mingled with sorrow. The moment held everything that mattered: love, responsibility, and the grace to say goodbye.

. . .

Recognising When It's Time - Quality of Life and the MEDW Criteria

To love a horse deeply is to carry the responsibility of knowing when their suffering has become too great. Euthanasia, as defined by the *University of Florida Extension*, is the humane ending of a horse's life to minimise pain and distress. It is an act of stewardship and compassion, the last kindness we can offer when comfort is no longer possible.

Veterinarians often use the *MEDW* criteria to help owners make this painful decision.

• **Movement:** Can the horse rise and walk without significant pain?

• **Eating:** Is appetite still strong, or has interest in food faded?

• **Drinking:** Is hydration normal?

• **Weight:** Has the horse lost twenty percent or more of its body mass?

These observations, taken daily, reveal changes that love alone can sometimes overlook. But physical signs are only part of the picture. Emotional well-being matters too. Horses that can no longer engage, that show fear, anxiety, or withdrawal, may be signalling that their quality of life has diminished.

Recognising these signs does not mean love has failed. It means love is strong enough to face truth with compassion.

. . .

Reasons and Considerations for Euthanasia

There are many reasons owners face this decision: incurable disease, chronic pain, severe injury, inoperable colic, or the simple frailty of old age. Sometimes the choice arises from safety concerns—a horse whose unpredictable behaviour poses danger—or from practical limitations, when care demands exceed physical or financial capacity

What matters most is honest conversation with your veterinarian. Signs that a horse may be nearing the end include persistent pain unrelieved by medication, dramatic weight loss, loss of appetite, and retreat from companionship. Often, owners sense subtle changes before anyone else does - the way the horse no longer greets them at the gate, or stands with head low in quiet resignation.

Listening to these cues is part of the bond we share. They speak softly, but they speak truth.

The Procedure - Compassion in Action

The act itself is mercifully peaceful. The veterinarian administers a sedative, easing the horse into deep calm. Then comes an overdose of anaesthetic, which brings rapid unconsciousness and a quiet passing There is no struggle, only stillness.

Owners are encouraged to stay if they wish, to stroke a familiar muzzle or whisper gratitude. Veterinarians confirm the absence of heartbeat and give time for farewell. Planning ahead for the horse's remains - burial, cremation, or removal -

helps ease the process and allows the owner to focus on the moment rather than logistics.

It is one of the hardest things a person can do. Yet within it lies an act of grace: a final gift of dignity, freely given in love.

The Heart Horse - Honouring Deep Bonds

Every rider has one - the heart horse. The one who carried them through seasons of change, who listened when words failed, who taught them patience and forgiveness. Losing such a companion can feel like losing part of oneself.

Grief after euthanasia can be intense and isolating. Many people feel anger, guilt, or disbelief when others do not understand the depth of their loss. It helps to honour the bond in tangible ways: create a photo album, frame a braid of mane, plant a tree in their memory, or write a letter of thanks. Rituals do not erase grief, but they give it form, transforming pain into remembrance.

Support matters too. Seek out friends, counsellors, or equine bereavement groups who understand that this is not "just an animal." It is the loss of a partner who carried your fears, your laughter, your dreams. Allow space for the sorrow, for it is proof of the love that was real.

Grief in Horses - Supporting the Herd Left Behind

Horses grieve as well. When a herd member dies, those left behind often show signs of distress - calling, pacing, standing watch at the empty stall. Some refuse food or withdraw into lethargy; others cling to remaining companions or to their humans for comfort.

The best support is steady routine. Keep feeding times and turnout schedules consistent. Offer quiet companionship, and ensure that surviving horses have social contact. Many experts suggest allowing herd members to approach and sniff the body if possible. It helps them understand the loss and reduces anxiety.

Watching a herd adjust to absence reminds us of our shared capacity to heal. Just as horses lean on one another, so too must we lean on our own communities. Grief, whether human or equine, softens when held together.

Letting Go and Moving Forward - Lessons in Acceptance

Choosing euthanasia is an act of profound courage. It demands that we set aside our own need to hold on and instead honour our horse's need for peace. The *University of Florida Extension* calls it an act of love, not surrender.

Grief has no set timeline. It may return in unexpected waves—the sight of an empty halter, the sound of hooves in memory. Accept each wave with gentleness. Speak your horse's name often. Tell their stories. Healing does not mean forgetting; it means carrying love forward in new ways.

Endings create space for beginnings. Another horse, another friendship, another chapter may come. The heart, once stretched by love, never returns to its former size. It becomes wider, more tender, and more capable of grace.

. . .

Dismounting with Grace

The pasture is quiet now. The last light fades from the hills, and the air smells of hay and rain. I walk to the gate, one hand on the worn leather reins that will soon be set aside. My horse stands still, eyes half closed, his breath steady and calm.

I press my cheek to his neck one final time and whisper words of thanks—thank you for carrying me, for teaching me, for waiting when I was afraid. His ears flick once, as if he understands. Then I step back, releasing the reins, watching as he drifts toward the far fence where the sky meets the earth.

The barn feels different afterward - quieter, larger somehow. But within that silence lies everything he gave me: patience, balance, trust, and the courage to begin again.

This is what it means to dismount with grace - to honour what was, to let love remain, and to carry its light forward.

Even in endings there is growth. Even in loss there is life. The lessons horses teach us - about hope, presence, and the strength found in gentleness - do not end when the ride does. They live on, steady as hoofbeats in memory, guiding us through whatever paths lie ahead.

And somewhere, just beyond the horizon, I like to imagine that my horse is still running - free, whole, and waiting for me at the edge of the dawn.

www.ingramcontent.com/pod-product-compliance
Lightning Source LLC
Chambersburg PA
CBHW051249020426
42333CB00025B/3127